C U :
G h o :

Prepare to be frightened by these terrifying tales from
around Cumbria

BRADWELL
BOOKS

Published by Bradwell Books
9 Orgreave Close Sheffield S13 9NP
Email: books@bradwellbooks.co.uk

British Library Cataloguing in Publication Data: a catalogue
record for this book is available from the British Library.

1st Edition
ISBN: 9781902674759

Print: Gomer Press, Llandysul, Ceredigion SA44 4JL

Design by: jenksdesign@yahoo.co.uk

Picture Credits: ShutterStock
and the author

CONTENTS

The wild and dramatic countryside of the Lake District is steeped in ghostly legends. Windermere is not only Cumbria's largest lake but its shores are among the most haunted.

INTRODUCTION

The modern county of Cumbria is made up of the ancient counties of Cumberland and Westmorland and incorporates a chunk of northern Lancashire. It is widely regarded as one of the most scenically beautiful counties in England, thanks to its dramatic mountain landscape punctuated by its celebrated lakes. The Lake District is a National Park attracting millions of visitors a year.

The Lake District was first made famous in the early days of British tourism by the Cumbrian poet William Wordsworth. Wordsworth's glorious evocations of the countryside he loved coincided with a growing appreciation of scenery and a vogue for the picturesque. His poems helped to attract hundreds and in time thousands of visitors to the Lake District, a fact which gave him anything but satisfaction: he considered the crowds of tourists unsightly and vulgar.

Cumbria is such a wild county, however, that even today in the height of summer there are many quiet and untrodden places to be found where its grandeur and romance seem unaffected. Some of these places are haunted by more than just the curlew and the buzzard.

Cumbria is also a historic county. It has been fought over by Romans and Ancient Britons, English and Scots, medieval kings and warlords, and Cavaliers and Roundheads. Among the remnants of all this border warfare are simple, square medieval fortifications known locally as 'pele towers'. A remarkable number of these have survived because they form the oldest parts of houses which have developed from them. Cumbria boasts more than its share of medieval manor houses, and many of these, too, are haunted.

All this history is guaranteed to inspire ghost stories and there are ghosts galore in Cumbria. They include celebrities such as Mary, Queen of Scots, several kings and Tom Skelton, one of England's most famous jesters, who may well have added the word 'tomfoolery' to the dictionary. Then there are the more anonymous spooks: murderers or their victims, soldiers, brides, miners, gypsies, cottagers, lords and numerous ladies known by the colour of their gowns, be they white, black, pink or grey. Some are very strange: animal ghosts; headless ghosts; disembodied screams and cries; the 'Radiant Boy' and the 'Cauld Lad'; shadowy armies on the mountain tops; and skulls that just won't stay buried. There is even a tale of a Cumbrian vampire.

The ghost stories of so many of Cumbria's lakes, mountains and stately homes add a dimension of mystery to this most romantic of counties.

THE CALGARTH SKULLS

Calgarth Hall is an ancient house, now a stud farm, situated near the shores of Lake Windermere. Today it is free of ghosts but once upon a time it was considered the most haunted house in the Lake District. The legend behind all the ghostly activity was that a former owner of the manor house, Myles Phillipson, framed two of his poorer neighbours, Mr and Mrs Cook, so that he could get his hands on their property. He invited them to Christmas dinner and had a servant hide a valuable silver cup in one of their coats. The cup was 'discovered' and the Cooks were promptly arrested. Because Phillipson was the magistrate, the Cooks' protestations were ignored and, after a mockery of a trial, they were hanged. On the gallows, however, Dorothy Cook cursed Phillipson, assuring him that his impious deed would not go unpunished.

Soon after the Cooks' murder – for such we may indeed call it – two skulls mysteriously appeared in the hall. They were presumed to be those of the Cooks but no one dared dig up their bodies to find out. At any rate, they were no ordinary skulls. Thinking someone was playing an ugly joke on him, Myles Phillipson angrily threw them out. When he returned to the hall, the skulls were waiting for him. Hardly able to credit his senses, he took them up again and hurled them far out into Lake Windermere. Stomping back, he was appalled to see them grinning at him in welcome through a front window. Not only had they got 'home' before him, they were literally bone dry. An icy chill now clutching his heart, Phillipson took up the skulls and bashed them to pieces with a hammer. Then he scattered the pieces in the lake. Even this drastic action proved in vain.

Nothing he could do would rid him of the skulls. He smashed them, burned them, crushed them to powder, scattered them to the winds and buried them far, far from Calgarth. But whatever he tried, moments later the headbones would be back, intact, and grinning sardonically from their accustomed place in the window.

All did not now go well with Myles Phillipson. The skulls' mute presence told their own story of the wrongdoing done to the Cooks. Shame and guilt weighed upon his conscience and he lost his former authority over the district. Bad luck blighted all his endeavours, and disease and other disasters destroyed his crops and killed his livestock. Not only that, but it was believed he passed very restless nights at Calgarth. The skulls were said to float about the hall of their own accord and wail and moan at all hours of the night, sometimes accompanied by weird lights and other spectres.

In time Phillipson's fortunes had collapsed to the point where he had to quit Calgarth Hall. He died in poverty, a broken man. The estate was bought by a Bishop of Llandaff who reverently reburied the skulls and exorcised the house. Peace reigned at Calgarth Hall ever after. (The Bishop found the house too cramped for his lavish lifestyle, though, and later built the grand Calgarth Park for himself on a nearby hill. This handsome Georgian estate has now been converted into flats).

The skulls of his two victims returned from the grave to condemn the squire of
Calgarth Hall, whose evil scheme had led to them being wrongly executed for theft.
erllre74/Shutterstock

THE CRIER OF CLAIFE

Today the ferry across Lake Windermere is a tourist attraction but in days gone by ferries were essential for travellers and farmers. A ferry trip could save hours of journeying along winding, muddy roads. Rawlinson Nab was one of the departure and landing points. It can be found on the Ordnance Survey map on the west bank of the lake, below Storrs and roughly opposite Ghyll Head. Coming from the east bank, the hills of Claife can be seen to tower above Rawlinson Nab. Centuries ago the Nab was haunted by a weird, invisible entity which became known as 'The Crier of Claife'.

The classic travel book, *The Complete Guide to the English Lakes* by Harriet Martineau, published in 1855, introduced this ominous being in print. She relates the following story:
'It was about the time of the Reformation, one stormy night, when a party of travellers were making merry at the Ferry-house, that a call for the boat was heard from the Nab. A quiet, sober boatman obeyed the call, though the night was wild and fearful. When he ought to be returning, the tavern guests stepped out upon the shore, to see whom he would bring. He returned alone, ghastly and dumb with horror. Next morning, he was in a high fever; and in a few days he died, without having been prevailed upon to say what he had seen. For weeks after, there were shouts, yells, and howlings at the Nab, on every stormy night: and no boatman would attend to any call after dark.'

There has been a long tradition of hermits living in isolation on the islands in Windermere and it so happened that a monk from Furness Abbey was in retreat on one of them at the time. A

*The ferry across Windermere. Hundreds of years ago ferrymen on Windermere
became terrified by a weird wailing entity which became known as
'The Crier of Claife'.*
David Johnstone-Wright/Shutterstock

party rowed out to see him and he agreed to do his best to
exorcise the evil spirit they presumed had taken up residence on
Rawlinson Nab. On Christmas Day on Chapel Island he
gathered together the local people and performed a service in
order to bind the spirit to a quarry in a nearby wood. It would
seem, however, that the exorcism was only partly successful, for
there are later stories of 'The Crier of Claife' wailing over
Windermere as an omen of doom. One story says that he was
heard just before a wedding party drowned in the lake on its
return from Hawkshead Church. The implication in this tale is
that 'The Crier' did not simply warn of the tragedy: it somehow
caused it.

11

WEDDING FOR THE DEAD

One of the weirdest and most dramatic ghost stories from Cumbria centres on Lake Thirlmere. The lake is now a reservoir, much more extensive than formerly, and the village of Armboth lies beneath its waters. Tradition has it Thirlmere became haunted after a bridal party tempted fate by holding their nuptials on All Hallows' Eve. The wedding feast took place at Armboth House beside the lake but the festivities were interrupted by horror when the bride's body was found strangled to death and floating in the water. It was presumed a jealous lover had killed her out of spite but the mystery was never solved. The tragedy cast such a pall over the family that they abandoned the house and never returned to it.

One Hallowe'en night many years later, those living nearby were surprised to see deserted Armboth House lit up and the cheerful sounds as of a party drifted to them across the lake. Two men crept up to the window to see who was in residence. They saw a long table being laid as if for a banquet but no guests were visible: instead the food, cutlery and chairs were moving about by themselves. Recollecting that it was the anniversary of the doomed wedding, the watchers took fright and ran away.

In subsequent years the phantom wedding party became more and more noisy and riotous. Bells would ring out and the murdered bride would emerge from her watery grave, shortly to be joined by her long-dead groom and the other ghostly guests. In addition, for some reason never explained, a huge black dog would be seen to swim across Thirlmere to join in the fun. Even the Calgarth Skulls would make an appearance. It has been well over a century, however, since the grim wedding party has been either seen or heard at Armboth.

No good came of a wedding held on the shores of Thirlmere on the fateful date of October 31 – Hallowe'en. The ghosts of the long-dead wedding party continued to haunt the area for many years afterwards.
Stewart Smith Photography/Shutterstock

The ghost of a young bride whose body was found floating in Thirlmere returned to haunt the scene of her murder every Hallowe'en night for many years.
Olena Zaskochenko/Shutterstock

THREE MORE HAUNTED LAKES

An odd and rather sad legend is told about Burnmoor Tarn, a small lake below Eskdale Fell. On a bleak winter's afternoon the body of a young man was being taken on the back of a pony across the moors to Wasdale, where he was to be buried. On the path beside the tarn the horse inexplicably took fright and bolted. It ran away so swiftly that the mourners soon lost sight of it in the gathering gloom. It was an even sadder procession that made its way home. Here they had the distressing task of telling the dead man's elderly mother what had happened. The shock was too much for her: she broke her heart with grief and passed away just a few days later.

Shortly afterwards, therefore, a second cortege made its way over Burnmoor, this time transporting the body of the old woman. And again, for reasons unknown, the pony bearing the corpse suddenly bolted near the tarn. It galloped away into the mountain mists. The appalled mourners hurried after it but stumbled hopelessly about in the fog until, to their amazement, they came across the pony they had lost on the previous occasion. It was quietly cropping the coarse yellow grass, the coffin containing the young man's body strapped to its back. The funeral party made the best of a bad job: they continued on to Wasdale and there buried the son. But the pony bearing the body of his mother was never recovered: she never received a decent burial.

From time to time, walkers caught in stormy or foggy weather on that lonely path past Burnmoor Tarn claim to have been almost run down by a shadowy horse. It thunders out of the twilight, a dark shape jolting crazily about on its back, before vanishing again into the gloom.

Local author H C Ivison, in her *Supernatural Cumbria* (Amberley 2010), records an equally eerie apparition from Loweswater: a trio of nuns apparently carrying a corpse. The body is wrapped in a shroud. This grim procession has been seen on moonlit nights slowly making its way down a road which skirts the lake. Their presence is a mystery. Although tradition states that a monastery may have been located in the Loweswater valley, there is no evidence of a nunnery being founded here.

Ms Ivison acknowledges a fellow writer, Denise Crellin, for helping to uncover another ghost in the vicinity of Loweswater. The scene is a single-track road that leads up to the hamlet of Mosser, situated above the lake. There are two versions of the story to account for the haunting: in each a young woman becomes pregnant and is abandoned by her husband; in one she is a clergyman's daughter, in the other the daughter of a cold-hearted man who refused to allow her to have any suitors and who turfed her out of the house even before she found herself with child. Whatever the truth of the story, the result was tragically the same: the poor girl hanged herself from a tree along the track to Mosser. The apparition of her lifeless body is said to still be glimpsed, dangling from a rope.

A second ghost may haunt this track. It is said to be that of a girl who was galloping along when she was thrown from her horse, breaking her neck. However, this tale may be a half-forgotten variant of the previous story and both ghosts may well be the same.

Several ghosts have been encountered near Loweswater, including the eerie apparition of nuns carrying a shrouded corpse.
Kevin Eaves / Shutterstock

Wast Water or Wastwater (either variant seems equally acceptable) is also haunted by a melancholy lady. This apparition, described as 'a woman in crinoline', is believed to have been Isobell Rowston, who a century-and-a-half ago lived in nearby Wasdale Hall. Isobell was driven out of her mind with grief after her little girl drowned in the freezing waters of Wastwater. Her ghost is said to be seen making its way from Wasdale Hall down to the lakeside, where it casts about desperately, as if searching still for her lost child. Occasionally Isobell has also been seen on Whin Rigg overlooking Wastwater. Perhaps she originally climbed up there to get an overview of the lake when looking for her missing daughter. Her unhappy spirit is also said to haunt Wasdale Hall.

PHANTOM WOMEN OF THE FALLS

Aira Force is one of the scenic highlights of the Lake District, a dramatic and beautiful waterfall that tumbles down to Ullswater, sparkling over picturesque rocks and ferns. It is now in the care of the National Trust and has been a destination for nature lovers since the early days of Cumbrian tourism. One lady tourist had an extraordinary experience here in the early 19th century. Her adventure was reported by Thomas De Quincey in his *Recollections of the Lake Poets*.

The lady in question, a Miss Smith, was determined to sketch the Force but foolishly went without a guide. Not content with sketching it from its lowest level, she scrambled up the side of the waterfall for a good half-hour in order to find the ideal composition. However, she was not an experienced climber, and had failed to take sensible note of either the route or her surroundings, with the result that she found herself trapped in what De Quincey describes as an 'aerial dungeon'. Further scrambling eventually freed her from her stony prison but her position became even more dangerous: Miss Smith found herself perched on a narrow ledge over a chasm. The rocks 'stood round her in a semi-circus, all lofty, all perpendicular, all glazed with trickling water, or smooth as polished porphyry'. She was in a terrible fix and could see no way out of her predicament.

Just then, however, she was surprised to see the figure of a woman dressed all in white beckoning to her from a narrow path snaking up the cliff. How the woman came to be there Miss Smith could not fathom, neither could she understand how she had failed to see the escape route now being indicated to her. With great caution and keeping her face and hands close to the slippery rock, Miss Smith followed the mysterious figure in white until she reached the other side of Aira Force and comparative safety. At that point she dared to look up. She was astonished to discover that her rescuer was her own sister! Failing to acknowledge her shouts of welcome, the woman in white continued to pick her way down beside the falls, Miss Smith gingerly following some distance behind until they reached the path which led to Ullswater. There the woman vanished. When a very relieved but puzzled Miss Smith arrived back at her lodgings, she found her sister waiting for her. Her sister confirmed she had not left the house all day.

Aira Force features in another ghostly legend, although there is some doubt as to its authenticity. It was made famous by William

Wordsworth in one of his poems, 'The Somnambulist', but there is some evidence he made up the story. It's believed he was told of an artist who had had been disturbed in the night by a sleepwalker while staying at Lyulph's Tower, a gothic hunting lodge built into the remains of a medieval castle. This is not entirely certain, however, and the legend has been retold for centuries.

According to the story, a beautiful girl called Emma once lived in the castle and she was betrothed to Sir Eglamore, a brave knight who had gone abroad to fight in some foreign war or other. Months went by without any word of her noble lover, and poor Emma began to pine. So distressed did she become that, unknown to anybody, including herself, Emma began to sleepwalk. Every night her sleeping form would leave the Tower and find its way to the place where she and Sir Eglamore used to meet, and where they had said their last farewell, a leafy bower beside the boiling waters of Aira Force. Eventually Sir Eglamore returned. He made his way to the castle up the path beside the waterfall and there spied a white-robed woman picked out in the moonlight. She was dropping leaves into the water. As he approached, Sir Eglamore realised it was his beloved Emma and he sprang forward with a cry of joy, touching her on the shoulder. Emma awoke startled. In her confusion she jumped away from Sir Eglamore and fell backwards into the rushing torrent.

The horrified Sir Eglamore dived in after her but was unable to save her. It was a miracle that he himself did not drown. Ever since the tragedy, it is claimed, Emma's white-clad ghost has been seen forlornly wandering around Aira Force.

*A tragic accident led to one of the ghosts seen at Aira Force. Another,
by contrast, probably prevented a tragedy.*
David Hughes/Shutterstock

Lakeland poet William Wordsworth is credited with inventing the story of Emma, the sleepwalking girl who fell to her death in Aira Force. However, this fails to explain why people have reported seeing her ghost.
Georgios Kollidas/Shutterstock

THE RADIANT BOY AND THE CAULD LAD

Corby Castle, near Carlisle, had – or perhaps still has – a ghost that is as enigmatic as it is famous. This is the so-called 'Radiant Boy'. The Victorian ghost story collector Catherine Crowe brought this unusually beautiful but apparently terrifying apparition to the world's attention in her book *The Night Side of Nature*. Crowe was a friend of the family who owned the castle and from the lady of the house she received a detailed report of the Radiant Boy, which included extracts from her journal. The extract dated September 8, 1803, has one of the best accounts of an appearance by the Radiant Boy:

'Amongst other guests invited to Corby Castle [she writes], came the Rev Henry A— of Redburgh, and rector of Greystoke, with his wife. According to previous arrangements, they would remain with us some days; but then this was cut short in a very unexpected manner. On the morning after their arrival we were all assembled at breakfast, when a chaise and four dashed up to the door in such haste that it knocked down part of the fence of my flower-garden. Our curiosity was, of course, awakened to know who could be arriving at so early an hour; when, happening to turn my eyes towards Mr A—, I observed that he appeared extremely agitated. "It is our carriage!" said he. "I am very sorry, but we must absolutely leave you this morning."

'We actually felt and expressed considerable surprise, as well as regret, at this unexpected departure; representing that we had invited Colonel and Mrs S—, some friends with whom Mr A— particularly desired to meet, to dine with us on that day. Our expostulations, however, were in vain; the breakfast was no sooner over than they departed, leaving us in consternation to conjecture what could possibly have occasioned so sudden an alteration in their arrangements. I really felt quite uneasy lest anything should have given them offence; and we reviewed all the occurrences of the preceding evening, in order to discover, if an offence that there was, whence it had arisen. But our pains were in vain; and after talking a great deal about it for some days, other circumstances managed the matter from our minds. It was not till we sometime afterwards visited the part of the county in which Mr A— resides, that we learned the real cause of his sudden departure from Corby. The real relation of the fact, as it here follows, is in his own words:

"'Soon after we went to bed, we fell asleep: it might be between one and two in the morning when I woke. I observed that the fire was totally extinguished; but although that was the case, and we had a light, I saw a glimmer in the centre of the room, which suddenly increased with bright flame.

"'I looked out, apprehending that something had caught fire; when, to my amazement, I beheld a beautiful boy, clothed in white, with bright locks resembling gold, standing by my bedside, in which position he remained some minutes, fixing his eyes upon me with a mild and benevolent expression. He then glided gently towards the side of the chimney, where it is obvious there was no possible egress, and entirely disappeared. I found myself again in total darkness, and all remained quiet until the usual hour of rising. I declare this to be a true account of what I saw at Corby Castle, upon my word as a clergyman.'"

This extraordinary little ghost is lacking any story to explain him: who he was in life and why he should haunt Corby Castle remains a mystery. Another 'Radiant Boy' is known. This apparition appeared to Robert Stewart, Lord Castlereagh, possibly in Ireland (the exact location is debated). He was told the boy's appearance was an omen, that those who saw it would rise to great power but would die an ignominious death. Lord Castlereagh became Chief Secretary for Ireland but ended his life through suicide in 1822.

Corby Castle, sketched in the early 1900s: home of the strange little ghost known as the Radiant Boy.

A not dissimilar but certainly more tragic ghostly child haunted Gilsland, at what is now the Gilsland Spa Hotel. This was the 'Cauld Lad'. According to legend, he was the spirit of a small boy who perished from cold thanks to the cruel treatment of his guardian. He haunted the family ever after, appearing as an omen of sickness or death. He would come 'shivering to their bedsides … his teeth audibly chattering' before illness set in and, if it were to prove fatal, he went one step further by 'laying his icy hand upon the part which would be the seat of the disease'. Then he would intone the mournful and reproachful words:

Cauld, aye cauld,
An ye'se be cauld for evermair!

He too has a duplicate, the Cauld Lad of Hylton Castle in
County Durham, but this Cauld Lad is more fairy than ghost.
Referring to the Radiant Boy of Corby Castle, Charles Harper,
in his classic work on *Haunted Houses* published in 1907, writes:
'Apparitions of this type are familiar in German spirit-lore and
are traditionally said, in the fearful mysticism which
characterises ancient Teutonic legends, to be the ghosts of
children murdered by their mothers – the *kindermörderinn* so
frequently mentioned in the folklore of Germany. A possible
explanation of a similar class of apparition being found in
Cumberland may be sought in the well-ascertained fact of the
district having been peopled in the ninth and tenth centuries by
settlers from Teutonic and Scandinavian countries, who would
naturally bring their folklore with them.'

If Harper is right, his theory might just as well explain the
presence of the Cauld Lad in Cumbrian legend.

OLD SHEPHERD AND PEG SNEDDLE

Traditional ghosts often do not appear as they used to in life. They can take on a number of different forms and often appear to belong as much to fairylore as they do to the realm of ghosts. In the old counties of Cumberland and Westmorland such ghosts were often referred to as 'boggles', a regional variant of the Lancastrian 'boggarts', the Welsh 'bwganau' and the transatlantic 'boogey-' or 'bogey-man'. When a well-known character in the village of Appleby-in-Westmorland known as Old Shepherd died, he returned as a boggle and made such a nuisance in his former home that a priest was called in to exorcise him. Although this succeeded in evicting him, it meant that Old Shepherd now had the run of the countryside. He could turn up anywhere, in a variety of shapes, including an indeterminate 'large white something', and liked nothing more than to alarm benighted travellers.

Old Shepherd was not the only ghost to haunt the countryside round Appleby. Another was 'Peg Sneddle', whose identity is uncertain but who may have been in life one Margaret Sledall of Crackenthorpe Hall. Peg would trundle around the local lanes in a carriage lit with amber lanterns, vanishing near a place called Peg Sneddle's Trough. She may have been the folk memory of some pre-Christian nature spirit for she was said to become angry in stormy weather but benign in fine weather. In other accounts she is presented as a kind of banshee of the Machell family of Crackenthorpe. Before death or misfortune befell a Machell, she would manifest either in the Hall itself or under an old oak tree, where she would be seen sitting and weeping.

BAD LORD LONSDALE

Lowther Castle, at Askham near Penrith, is a grand country house boasting magnificent gardens. Abandoned in the 1930s, it recently underwent an extensive restoration project after falling into a serious state of disrepair and is now open to the public.

Lowther Hall, to give it its original name, was built in the late 17th century by the first Lord Lonsdale, who was known as Jemmy Lowther. According to John Ingram, the author of *Haunted Homes and Family Legends*, published in the 1880s, Lowther was a 'notorious character' whose brutal ways earned him the name of 'Bad Lord Lonsdale'. Worse still, says Ingram,

A 19th-century engraving of Lowther Hall, home to the first Lord Lonsdale, whose ghost terrorised the neighbourhood.

*Walla Crag, overlooking Derwent Water. Under this distinctive crag the
unruly spirit of 'Bad Lord Lonsdale' was imprisoned.*
mandy willett/Shutterstock

he proved 'a still greater terror to the neighbourhood after death than he had ever been during his life'. He returned as a ghost, and a very badly behaved one at that.

Even burying him was difficult. Bad Lord Lonsdale's ghost caused a rumpus at his interment. He shoved the clergyman praying over his body so hard that he nearly fell over. His spirit rested no more easily after his bones were laid in the grave.

'There were continual disturbances in the hall and noises in the stables,' writes Ingram, 'and neither men nor animals were suffered to rest. His Lordship's phantom coach and six is still remembered and spoken of, and still believed by some to be heard dashing across the country. Nothing is said of the "bad lord's" shape or appearance, and it is doubtful whether the spectre has ever appeared to sight, but it has frequently made itself audible. The hall became almost uninhabitable on account of the dead man's pranks, and out of doors was, for a long time, almost equally dreaded, as even there there was constant danger of encountering the miscreant ghost.'

Eventually, Bad Lord Lonsdale's spirit was 'laid' (i.e. exorcised) under a huge outcrop of rock called the Walla Crag and since then Lowther Castle and the country round have been free of his unnerving presence.

MURDERS AT MUNCASTER

Muncaster Castle is a handsome fortified manor house, open to the public and happy to promote its haunted heritage. 'Ghost sits' and overnight vigils are regularly held. One of its traditional ghosts is Tom Skelton, court jester here at the end of the 1500s. Peter Frost-Pennington, at the castle, told the local press: 'Many people are pretty sure he's still here, playing tricks. I didn't believe in ghosts when I came here. But if you think you're getting good at something, the Fool pricks your pomposity. You'll be showing people around and equipment will stop working. One or two people who perhaps haven't been very pleasant while they've been here have reported being shaken in their beds. They shouldn't have been so nasty the day before.'

One of the abiding legends of 'Tom Fool' is that he was given a grim commission by his master, Sir Ferdinand Pennington, to get rid of a young carpenter who had formed a misalliance with his daughter Helwise. No jolly jape this. Sir Ferdinand was horrified at the idea of a romance between Helwise and a 'lowly' craftsman. Skelton understood that the carpenter was to be done away with permanently and took his commission seriously. He used the carpenter's own axe to murder him. Skelton then hacked off the head and presented it to Sir Ferdinand as proof that the deed was done. According to author Jack Hallam, the headless ghost of the unlucky carpenter haunts Muncaster along with that of Tom Skelton.

A royal phantom also graces Muncaster with its presence. This is the spirit of King Henry VI, who found sanctuary with the Penningtons when he briefly became a fugitive after a serious

*Historic Muncaster Castle boasts a number of ghosts, including that of the
original Tom Fool, whose antics were not always amusing.*
Kevin Eaves/Shutterstock

*The spirit of King Henry VI of England is one of Cumbria's
more regal ghosts.*

defeat during the War of the Roses. Before he reached Muncaster many other doors had been closed against him out of fear. He never forgot the kindness shown to him by the Penningtons and among other privileges he presented them with a beautiful glass drinking vessel, ornamented with gold and enamel, which became known as the Luck of Muncaster. It is thought that the comparative calm and serenity Henry experienced at Muncaster during his turbulent life is what tempts his spirit to linger here again.

In addition to this impressive roster of spooks, Muncaster Castle also boasts a traditional lady in white. This White Lady haunts the grounds and roads around the castle and is said to be the shade of Mary Bragg, a girl who was murdered near the main entrance.

According to the current owners, the most haunted place in Muncaster Castle itself is the Tapestry Room, where many visitors have experienced disturbed nights. They have reported seeing the door handle turned by invisible hands and hearing the sound of a child crying near the window, sometimes accompanied by woman's voice, soothingly singing.

FOUR MORE HAUNTED CASTLES

Dacre Castle, south-west of Penrith, is an archetypal castle in miniature: square, stone-built, with a castellated tower at each corner. It dates back to the 15th century and, after a considerable restoration programme in the 1960s, is now a private residence (although it is easily viewable from a footpath which passes by it). A horrible legend pertains to this little fortress: that an unfaithful Lady Dacre found herself shut away in one small room for the rest of her life, her only companion the embalmed corpse of her lover. She is not the ghost, however. The apparitions of Dacre Castle are true VIPs: three kings, no less. They are Owain of Cumbria, Athelstan of England and Constantine of Scotland. They met here in the 10th century to sign what today we might call a non-aggression pact. They are said to be seen patrolling the grounds in peaceful discourse – despite the fact that within weeks of the conference the peace broke down and they were at each other's throats again.

Also in the vicinity of Penrith is Greystoke Castle, another medieval castle but one greatly enlarged upon and gentrified since its first phase of wooden construction in the 11th century. Its appearance today is much more that of a manor house (and a very handsome one) than a fortress. There is a great mystery attached to Greystoke. Centuries ago, an aristocratic guest of the house failed to come down for breakfast and then lunch. A servant was dispatched to see if the man was ill. His bedroom was in the oldest part of the building still standing, the former pele tower. The servant found the room empty, the guest missing. He was indeed nowhere to be found. Greystoke was searched from top to bottom, the 6,000-acre park explored yard by yard and the ponds dragged. The missing guest failed to turn up again dead or alive.

Actually, that last statement is not quite true. For it is said that on the anniversary of his disappearance, the spirit of the missing man returns to haunt the chamber from which he vanished. I can only presume that no one has had the courage to ask the ghost what on earth happened to him, for the mystery of the missing guest remains a mystery still. It may just possibly be linked to the other ghost of Greystoke, for it would appear that this particular bedroom had already become known as 'the haunted room'. According to legend, a subterranean passage runs from the chapel in the grounds to the pele tower. In the bad old feudal days, a monk was punished by being trapped in this passage, with the exits at either end walled up, so that he died a cruel, lingering death in the dark. His frantic knockings are said to still be heard on the walls of the haunted bedroom. Did the missing guest somehow answer the calls of the ghostly knocks and himself get trapped along with the long-dead monk?

Shutting people away seems to have been a habit in Cumbria in the Middle Ages. Centuries ago the lord of Sizergh Castle, south of Kendal and now a National Trust property, decided to lock up his wife when he was called away to visit the king. He clearly didn't trust the unhappy woman for the chamber he chose for her incarceration was a tiny one in the depths of the castle rather than her usual bedroom; perhaps he feared she might be rescued by some lover, imagined or otherwise. He also gave strict instructions to his servants not to release their mistress from her chamber under any circumstances until his return.

Blood-curdling screams have been heard emanating from within the walls of Sizergh Castle, echoes of a horrible tragedy which occurred in the Middle Ages.
Kevin Eaves/Shutterstock

Terrified of their lord's displeasure, the servants followed his instruction to the letter. The door was never opened for the entire time he was away. No one thought to bring food to their unfortunate mistress and her pleas, screams and final gasps went ignored. Eventually, of course, she starved to death. Her desperate shrieks are still to be heard, it is said, echoing around the battlements, but it has proved impossible to determine where they emanate from. The locked room has never been found and some believe the skeleton of the abused woman still lies there.

Naworth Castle, north of Carlisle, is another spectacular medieval building, privately owned but often used for special events and even as a film set. The grounds are haunted by a traditional White Lady. She is a tragic figure, a young woman who was seduced by a lord of the manor in the 16th century, bearing him a son. The naive girl believed Lord Dacre would marry her but, because she was merely the daughter of one of his tenants, he had no intention of doing so and instead married a woman of a social status he considered more fitting. As he repeated his marriage vows in the chapel, the girl he had wronged drowned herself in the stream that runs through the estate. After the wedding Lord Dacre was strolling with his new bride through the grounds when they came to the stream – and saw the body of the dead girl, her hair splayed out on the water, her dead eyes staring accusingly up at them.

Before Lord Dacre could react, he heard a shrill cry from the opposite bank. It was the dead girl's mother. She cursed Lord Dacre with the words: 'May evil grim aye follow him, until the day he dee!' It could be argued that the curse worked, for Lord Dacre lived only a few more years and his only child and heir died when he fell off his rocking horse. The male line therefore came to an end, and to ensure that Lord Dacre's wickedness would not be forgotten the forlorn spirit of the drowned girl, in the form of the White Lady, began to haunt the environs of Naworth Castle.

THE GYPSY'S CURSE

Levens Hall, south of Kendal, is a grand Elizabethan manor house with world-renowned ornamental gardens. It is open to the public. The famous legend of Levens Hall involves a prophecy or curse (there are two versions) dependent on the birth of a pure white fawn among the herd of fallow deer in the park. In one version of the story, a starving gypsy woman called at the house but her pleas for food and shelter were ignored and she was scornfully turned away. Before she succumbed to her hunger and the elements, she cursed the owners of Levens Hall, the Bagots, proclaiming that their land would be dispersed to strangers and that no male heir would be born to them until a white doe was born on the estate and the River Kent had frozen over (it was obviously a long dying breath!). The curse is claimed to have been fulfilled and only broken in the bitter winter of 1896 when the Kent did indeed freeze, an albino doe was born to one of the deer and Mrs Bagot was delivered of the infant Alan Desmond.

A 'Grey Lady' haunts the drive leading up to Levens Hall and has been the cause of numerous accidents, stepping in front of carriages and more recently cars, causing them to swerve (on one occasion, however, a cyclist ploughed straight through her!).

A Grey Lady and a friendly little dog are among the ghosts of Levens Hall.
Kevin Eaves/Shutterstock

She has also been seen walking beside the A6, which passes close to the house. The Grey Lady has been identified with the spurned gypsy but this is a rather doubtful conclusion. She is often seen in company with a little black dog and it seems unlikely that a starving woman would be in possession of a pet. A similar ghostly animal, quite possibly the same one, has also been seen about the place, particularly on the main staircase. The late Mrs Annette Bagot, writing about the ghost in a guidebook published in the 1970s, described it as 'small and woolly, like an unclipped poodle with bright eyes'. She continued: 'I see it often. Sometimes when I open a door it runs out under my feet and I nearly trip over it. At times it follows me or it likes to sit and listen to my husband playing the harpsichord. Our own dogs often chase it.'

The current owners have also encountered the phantom pooch outside the house. A rather odd incident occurred while the late Robin Bagot was playing the harpsichord. He appears to have been in two places at once, for while he was clearly seen sitting at the instrument, he was also undoubtedly in Keswick at the time on business.

We are not through with the ghosts of Levens Hall yet. In addition to the rather sinister Grey Lady, there is also a Pink Lady. She seems a friendly soul and there is nothing about her to suggest she is anything but a living human being.

'She is dressed as an 18th-century maid,' writes Annette Bagot. 'Her pink skirt is looped at the waist, over what may be panniers, her mob cap always covers her face. She seems so real and solid [but] she suddenly vanishes like a figure on a television screen. She is just there one moment and then she's gone.'

On the Levens Hall website, the Bagots also report spooky atmospheres in the Small Drawing Room and the Bellingham Bedroom directly above it. They say that from time to time visitors have found the latter room so creepy that they refuse to sleep in it.

THE LUNATIC IN GREY

Lorton Hall, near Cockermouth, is a 17th-century manor which, like so many of Cumbria's stately homes, started life as a medieval pele tower. It is haunted by a Grey Lady whose history is something of a mystery, although there is a tradition to explain her presence. Veteran ghost-hunter, the late Andrew Green, received an interesting and informative letter from a former owner of the hall, the Revd J A Woodhead-Keith-Dixon, detailing what was known of the ghost. He understood that the Grey Lady had been a member of the family living at Lorton Hall in the 18th century. She was born with a mental condition that deteriorated through her life, so that she became 'gradually more and more insane'.

'We have a grave in the garden at the Hall, always supposed to be that of the Grey Lady,' the Revd Woodhead-Keith-Dixon told Andrew Green. 'The reason given for her being buried in the garden is that the then vicar refused to allow a lunatic to be buried in consecrated ground.

'The appearances are always closely connected with the full moon – opening and closing of doors between 5 and 7.30 in the morning. Only once, however, have I actually seen the apparition during one of these periods. This was at the unexpected time of 9.20am. I thought it was my wife coming down the stairs, as these were distinct feminine footsteps, and I went towards the library door to speak to her. All I saw was a grey gauzy figure carrying a lighted candle – completely ignoring me and going on down the corridor. I recovered quickly enough to get down the corridor in time to see the figure pass through the dining room window (where the front door used to be in the days when she lived in the house).

'The tenant of the home farm, who was a very down-to-earth old Cumbrian and not given to romancing in any way, said he had seen the ghost on several occasions and simply accepted her as a fact. At the end of the war a company of Girl Guides was allowed to camp in the grounds. They were packing up in the early hours of the morning when one of the Guides saw the ghost coming out of the front door and walking in the garden.' It is intriguing that the Grey Lady should be described as a lunatic and that she should only appear during the full moon, for the moon was anciently supposed to exert an influence on the insane – hence the 'luna' in 'lunatic'. In his communication with Green, the Revd Woodhead-Keith-Dixon adds one rather unnerving detail about this otherwise placid apparition. He told him:

'Only one attempt has been made to exorcise the ghost – in 1923 – but on the morning this was to be done the priest who was to officiate dropped dead. This was taken to be an indication that nothing should be done so nothing further has taken place since that time.'

Was the Grey Lady responsible?

CARLISLE'S CASTLE AND CATHEDRAL

Carlisle is an ancient settlement whose name stems from its Iron Age name Caer Luel, or 'The Fortress of Luel'. Luel appears to be a local variant on the name of the Celtic god Lugh. As a border town, Carlisle has been witness to much conflict, including clashes between Romans and Brigantes, Scots and English, Cavaliers and Roundheads and various medieval chieftains.

One of Carlisle's oldest buildings is its castle, dating back to the reign of King William II. Two men, a Lord Grey and his son-in-law, had an unsettling experience here one evening in 1818. They were strolling on the castle's ramparts when a man approached them, walked past, then approached them again before suddenly disappearing over the parapet. They recognised the shadowy figure as a man of both their acquaintance, a lawyer named Sir Samuel Romilly. Unbeknownst to either of them, Sir Samuel had killed himself that night by cutting his throat. Why his apparition should have appeared to them at the moment of his death remained a mystery to them both.

Carlisle Castle is the setting for that rarest of phenomena – a ghost killing a living person. In truth, it was the shock of encountering the phantom which caused the death rather than any violence perpetrated by the ghost itself. In 1835, when the castle was being greatly extended, with new barracks and the square being constructed, there was a grisly discovery. Walled up in the keep, a woman's skeleton was revealed, dressed in faded tartan with her bony feet resting on a piece of tartan silk.

That she had been a noblewoman was evident by the costly rings she wore. Many Scottish prisoners have been incarcerated in the castle, among them Mary, Queen of Scots and rebels during the Jacobite revolt. The identity of this unfortunate woman remains unknown but it is believed to be her ghost that drifts quietly around the precincts of the keep.

On one fateful night, a soldier on guard duty challenged her as she emerged out of the dark. As the eerie figure failed to respond and continued to approach him, the soldier took fright and lunged at her with his bayonet. Assuming she was a human intruder, he got a terrible fright when his bayonet passed right through her and she 'seemed to dissolve into the ground'. He too collapsed, and died a few hours later.

H C Ivison, in her *Supernatural Cumbria*, mentions another ghostly tradition of the castle, but recognises it may simply be a confusion of the story told above. This tells of a young woman who was 'bricked up' in a recess in the Captain's Tower by a cruel captain who had made her pregnant but didn't want anyone to know. She is now said to haunt the Captain's Tower, dressed all in white. Ivison states that 'a smiling Cavalier' also haunts Carlisle Castle (a Royalist garrison suffered a serious defeat here during the Civil War), and that the castle's greatest celebrity prisoner, Mary, Queen of Scots, is another phantom visitor.

The ghost of Mary of the Scots may also be encountered elsewhere in Carlisle. According to Darren Ritson's *Haunted Carlisle* (History Press 2012), she has been seen in Long Lane, which leads to the cathedral. Darren checked with noted

Carlisle Castle, where a soldier died of shock
after encountering a ghost.
Kevin Eaves/Shutterstock

Mary, Queen of Scots was interred in Carlisle Castle and her ghost is now said to haunt its environs.

authorities the Marie Stuart Society, who confirmed that although Mary was 'in protective custody' at Carlisle Castle, her royal status allowed her a number of privileges, which included strolls under armed guard to worship at the cathedral. It is not beyond the bounds of possibility, therefore, that she may have walked along Long Lane, giving at least some credence to alleged sightings of her.

Carlisle Cathedral itself is also haunted, but not by Mary. This comparatively modest building (the second smallest, after Oxford, of the ancient cathedrals of Britain) started life as a priory but became a cathedral as early as 1133. There are rumours of a haunted tunnel beneath the cathedral leading to Devonshire Street (it is remarkable how many churches have such stories told about them) but its better known spook story involves a bishop whose apparition started to 'walk' after his tomb was mucked about with. During remodelling work, it is said, the tombs of various past bishops of the cathedral were moved to a new position. This seemed to irritate the spirit of one of the bishops, for his shade began to manifest at the place where his sarcophagus now stood. It would then stalk through the cloisters to the spot where it had formerly rested. He would stand there glaring about him for a while and then vanish. The authorities took the hint and reinstalled the tombs in their original positions.

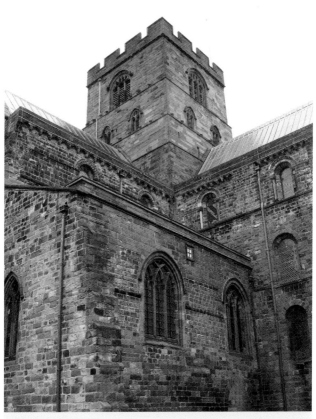

*The troubled spirit of a former bishop of Carlisle Cathedral made its presence
known after his tomb was disturbed.*
Collpicto/Shutterstock

MORE FROM CARLISLE

Gerald Findler, who wrote two books on Lakeland legends in the 1960s, recounted a personal experience of the supernatural while working as an orderly at a makeshift hospital in a Carlisle school during the First World War. Room was limited and a wounded soldier was made as comfortable as possible in a hut in the school's playground. This was an Australian sergeant named Chase who had been badly injured by shrapnel from an exploding bomb. One night, Findler crossed the playground to check on Sgt Chase and was surprised to see a light on in the hut. A lamp was brightly shining in the window. Findler opened the door and saw an elderly man sitting beside the bed holding Sgt Chase's hand. Findler smiled and said he'd come back later. Over a cup of tea with one of the nurses, Findler mentioned the man sitting with Sgt Chase. 'Visitors at this time of night? Never!' declared the nurse stoutly and she immediately headed over to the hut, Findler in tow. The hut was now in darkness. When the lamp was lit, it was seen that Sgt Chase was alone – and had died. When they were laying out his body and seeing to his personal effects, Findler came across several photographs. He immediately recognised one of them as the elderly man he had seen earlier. It was Sgt Chase's father.

A more startling apparition was seen in the former Citadel Restaurant (now the Old Arcadian Restaurant) in English Street. In 1966 a Mr Don Reid was waiting for a friend in one of the bars when he noticed someone standing in the entrance. He jumped up and began to cross to the bar in order to get his expected friend a drink. But then he realised his mistake. It wasn't his friend – it wasn't even human. Mr Reid stood amazed as 'a grey-black shape about 5ft 7in tall' but with no identifiable facial features walked towards him. A few feet away from him it 'seemed to disappear just as if it had been poured into the ground' (to quote author Andrew Green). A barmaid had also glimpsed the thing and went into an adjoining bar, expecting to find the 'customer' there: of course, it was empty.

Mr Reid was convinced the figure was that of a man. If so, then there is another ghost haunting the building. About a year after Mr Reid's sighting, the licensees' six-year-old child asked her mother about 'an old woman in grey' she had seen, thinking it was her babysitter. The apparitions may possibly have some connection with subterranean tunnels which run from the restaurant towards the former gaol over the road and, in the opposite direction, towards the cathedral. This can only be conjecture, however, for both spooks remain unidentified.

Another mystery which caused a bit of a stir in Carlisle was caught on CCTV in 2008 outside an off-licence in Botcherby. The footage shows a 'strange white mist' which enters the Simply Food & Drinks shop and then leaves again a number of times over the course of one evening. It approached the shop from over the road, where a flat was being renovated. Did the building work disturb a spirit, wondered the off-licence staff? If so, perhaps it was searching for spirits of a different kind to help it return to its long rest.

A place becoming firmly established on the commercial ghost-hunting map is Carlisle Citadel Railway Station, or rather the extensive suite of rooms beneath it, known as the Undercroft. The station was built in the 19th century and the Undercroft has been used in many different ways since then, from equipment stores to shops (in one room the hooks which belonged to a butcher's establishment are still to be seen fixed to the ceiling). Now it is used for 'ghost tours'.

Railway workers have reported all manner of strange noises in the labyrinthine passages and rooms and also doors opening and closing by themselves. Station manager Sue Howarth, who says she was once startled by an invisible 'icy finger' which poked her in the back of the neck, informed *Haunted Carlisle* author Darren Ritson of a considerable number of apparitions allegedly seen at the station. These include a small boy with a dog; a shadowy figure standing on a platform in a blizzard; a woman in a veil; and a man without his head. The latter two sound a little too good (or gruesome) to be true, for the story given to explain them is actually to be found in the second volume of the famous *Ghost Book* by Lord Halifax (Bles 1937) and the link with Carlisle is a tenuous one. But it's worth repeating:

'A Colonel Ewart was travelling alone by express train from Carlisle to London. He went to sleep and, when he woke up, found that a lady in black with a crape veil had entered his compartment and occupied one of the corner seats. As he had been asleep for some time, he supposed she must have entered rather quietly and apologised to her for being without his coat and his boots. The lady made no reply, and thinking she might be deaf and had not heard him, he crossed to the other side of the compartment and sat down in the seat opposite to her. He thought her conduct strange and was still wondering about it when there came a sudden crash. There had been a collision.

'Colonel Ewart was unhurt and at once jumped out to see if he could be of any use. Then, remembering the lonely lady in the compartment and wondering if she were frightened or injured, he went back. The carriage was empty; there was no trace of the lady anywhere; and the guard declared that the door had been locked, although the collision had forced it open, and that no one could possibly have come in since Carlisle, as the train had not stopped anywhere until the accident occurred.

'Later Colonel Ewart learnt that a few years before, a bride and bridegroom had been travelling on the same line and by a corresponding train. The man had put his head too far out of the window to look at something, and it had been caught by a wire, so that the headless body had fallen back into the carriage. At the next station the bride was found singing a lullaby over her husband's body. The shock had driven her completely mad.'

GHOSTS OF THE COAST

According to the late ghost-hunter Elliott O'Donnell, the waters of the Solway Firth are haunted by a number of spectral ships. One of these is said to appear as a warning of an imminent shipwreck. He writes: 'It is supposed to be the phantom of a vessel containing a bridal party that was maliciously wrecked in the Solway many years ago.' In addition, he claims that not one but two pirate ships, cursed because of their crews' crimes, are doomed to sail around the Firth until doomsday.

Another ghostly vessel associated with the Solway Firth is the *Betsy Jane*, a slave ship which crashed into the Giltstone Rock off

The waters of the Solway Firth are haunted by a number of spectral ships, including the slave ship Betsy Jane, which sank on Christmas Eve.
cieniu1/Shutterstock

Whitehaven. Returning from its evil trade, it sighted the Cumbrian coast on Christmas Eve and the church bells could be heard joyously pealing across the water. The cruel and greedy captain of the *Betsy Jane* laughed scornfully at the sound of the bells and announced that 'the bells could ring till they cracked, but it would be the chink of his gold that rang on Christmas morning'. This blasphemy tried the patience of the powers of Providence too far and his fate and that of his crew were sealed. The ship foundered against the Giltstone Rock and all hands were lost, their screams and wails drowned out by the ringing of the bells. At Christmas time, it is said, the *Betsy Jane* may still be seen, surging towards the Giltstone Rock, just as it did all those years ago.

Meanwhile the beach at Grange-over-Sands is said to be 'peopled by ghosts'. The sands here were a main crossing point over Morecambe Bay but were – and still are – treacherous and many have lost their lives over the centuries, caught in quicksand or by the rushing tide. Now, it is claimed, 'when the wind is from the sea [the sands] seem to be alive with the cries of drowning men and women'.

GHOSTS UNDERGROUND

Dr John Mason Neale, in his *The Unseen World* of 1853, writes of a haunted mine at Whitehaven. Several mines extended out from Whitehaven, exploring coal fields deep below the ocean waves. Narrow, cramped, suffocating, they were prone to accidents and, to quote Dr Neale, were 'some of the most terrible in England'. He explains that such dangerous working conditions encouraged a great deal of superstition among the colliers and reports of ghosts were not uncommon:

'A man who had worked all his life in [the mines], and had always borne high character, was laid on his death-bed, and sent for the

Ghosts have been seen at Whitehaven, both out to sea and, more unusually, in a mine deep below the town.
Brendan Howard/Shutterstock

clergyman of the parish, to whom he had been previously known. He assured the priest that it was no uncommon thing in the mines for the voices of persons who had long been dead to be heard as in conversation or debate. I do not think he said that apparitions were to be seen; but he affirmed that they were heard to pass along the passages with a loud kind of rushing noise; that the miners as far as possible got out of the way on these occasions; that the horses employed in the mines would stand still and tremble, and fall into a cold sweat, and that this was universally known to be a thing that might occur at any time.'

The dying man told the priest a remarkable story. He said a Cumbrian man who had worked for many years in the mines was found to be dishonest and dismissed from his job as overseer. He was allowed to continue working in an inferior role but the overseer's position went to a Northumbrian man. 'To this person', writes Dr Neale, 'the degraded overseer bore the strongest hatred, and was heard to say that some day he would be his ruin. He lived, however, in apparent friendship with him.'

One day the two men were killed by an explosion in a rarely visited gallery. The Cumbrian man, highly knowledgeable of the mine where he had been employed for so many years, would certainly have known that that part of the workings was notorious for 'fire-damp' (explosive gas) and yet it was afterwards found that he had entered the levels without a safety lamp. After the tragedy disembodied voices were sometimes heard in the gallery, raised 'high in dispute'. The voices were clearly recognisable as those of the two dead men. The presence of the ghost led the miners to ponder on what really happened that day. The conclusion they came to was that 'preferring revenge to life, the ex-overseer had taken his successor into a place where he knew the fire-damp to exist and had thus contrived his destruction'.

MORE OUT-OF-DOORS GHOSTS

Ulpha Old Hall is a ruined medieval manor house north of
Broughton-in-Furness. Its odd name is believed to come from
the Norse word for wolf. Tradition has it that a former lady of
the Old Hall found herself surrounded by wolves one day while
taking a stroll around her estate. In her panic she ran away down
the valley away from her home and was ultimately devoured by
the pack. Her unhappy ghost is said to still haunt the region.

A more aggressive female phantom has been encountered in the
vicinity of Askerton Castle, north of Brampton. Her name is

An engraving of a gibbet made in about the year 1800.
In Cumbria the sites of two of these grisly landmarks became haunted.

Bonnie May Marye and she was murdered by her lover. Hers is a very angry spirit. She has been known to pursue people, even those on horseback, down the lanes, only giving up when they pass over the parish boundary at Kirckcambeck. 'On another occasion,' states Jack Hallam in his *Ghosts of the North* (David & Charles 1976), 'she is reputed to have immobilised a rider by taking hold of his horse's bridle as he rode past and not letting go until the horseman had made a promise, which if divulged, would result in his death.'

An invisible but no less unnerving ghost was experienced by many people journeying by night along the road between Carlisle and Penrith in the vicinity of Barrock Park, near Southwaite. Jack Hallam suggests this was an 'old road' since removed by the construction of the M6 motorway, but to me the A6 seems more likely, for it was the old post road. The haunting took the form of blood-curdling screams and yells; chilling enough but rendered even more ghastly by knowledge of their origin. They belonged, it was said, to the ghost of notorious highwayman John Whitfield. Whitfield was such a terror to the neighbourhood and committed so many murders that when he was finally caught, he suffered the extreme penalty of being gibbeted alive. This meant he was hung in chains and starved to death. He was gibbeted close to where he committed his last robbery and it was from there that the eldritch cries were heard to emanate – years after he was put out of his misery by a bullet in the brain from a passing mail-coachman.

A gibbet also used to stand alongside what is now the A686, a mile or two west of Langwathby. A butcher named Tom Parker was murdered for the full purse he had accrued earlier that day at Penrith market. The killer turned out to be Parker's own godson, one Nicholson. He was promptly hanged and his body hung in chains near the spot where the crime was committed. For years Nicholson's body swung from the gibbet beside the road until it was nothing more than bones and rags. Eventually, the gibbet was blown down in a storm and a gang of local men buried the murderer's bones where they had fallen. Now, it is said, a ghostly gibbet haunts the site, a grisly skeleton swinging from its arm.

In contrast to these two villains, it is a benign and friendly ghost haunting the lanes around Cartmel. He is described as 'dressed in full John Bull garb, complete with curly brimmed topper, double-breasted waistcoat, breeches and ankle boots'. He has been encountered in daylight and is said to be most polite, opening gates for people and helping ladies over stiles!

Kirkstone Pass (now the A592) is one of the oldest and most important routes through Lakeland. In winter it can be a very bleak and forbidding place. It therefore took some courage for a young mother, Ruth Reay, to journey out into the snow just a few weeks after giving birth to her son. She had received the sad tidings that her father had fallen gravely ill and she was desperate not only to see him but to make sure he had seen his infant grandson, should the worst happen. This was the early 19th century, she was poor, and there was no other means to get to her father's sickbed than on her own two feet. Wrapping up herself and her baby as warmly as she could, she headed out into what rapidly became a blizzard.

Kirkstone Pass is haunted by a young mother who was caught in a snowstorm while struggling to reach the home of her dying father.
Kevin Eaves/Shutterstock

Poor Ruth didn't stand a chance: she stumbled through the blinding sleet and snow and the bitter, icy wind for as long as she was able but at last she succumbed, almost in sight of her destination, and shelter. The crying of her baby, kept warm by Ruth's body where she fell, alerted people to the tragedy but it was too late to save her. On winter's nights Ruth's shade has sometimes been seen staggering through the dark, clutching a bundle to her heart, and on occasions the thin wail of an infant in distress has also been heard.

On the summit of the steepest part of Kirkstone Pass (known as 'The Struggle') can be found a popular hostelry, the Kirkstone Inn. The inn is haunted by the spirit of a child, believed to be a coachman's boy called Neville who died when he was run over by a carriage. He is responsible for the mild poltergeist activity which occasionally plagues the pub and his cheeky face has been seen peering through a window. A phantom coachman – the grieving father, perhaps? – has also been glimpsed and possibly even photographed outside the inn. A nearby tree is claimed as the haunt of a woman who was hanged from it after she murdered her child and there are also vague rumours of a 'Grey Lady' haunting the vicinity.

Dunmail Raise is the name of the pass that used to divide the old counties of Cumberland and Westmorland. At the top of the pass, near where the A591 breasts the hill, there is a large mound – probably the 'Raise' itself – and in this, according to tradition (unfortunately unsupported by fact), is buried King Dunmail, Dark Age ruler of Cumberland. The legend continues that Dunmail's crown was thrown into a nearby tarn to prevent it getting into the wrong hands, but once a year a ghostly retinue of warriors fish it from out of the deep waters and carry it to the king's cairn. They tap thrice on the mound but so far a hollow voice has called out that 'it is not yet time' and the warriors have returned the crown to the tarn. Perhaps one year Dunmail will answer the call and be resurrected, but with no kingdom of Cumberland to rule, it's hard to know what job he could find to do.

Kathleen Ashbridge, a member of the Caldbeck and District Local History Society, has a notebook of her aunt's which refers to a ghost. In an entry dating from about 1910, the lady refers to a ghostly black dog which haunted a stretch of road at Branthwaite Neuk. She writes: 'It appears from a holly bush in the hedge, then disappears into one a little way off.'

Black Dogs are among the most commonly reported spooks in British folklore and yet they are among the most enigmatic. These are not the ghosts of domestic breeds (like the Grey Lady of Levens Hall's pet) but huge, monstrous beasts far larger than any living breed today and often sporting fiery red eyes. Seeing one was considered very unlucky, perhaps an omen of the witness's imminent death. One of these fearsome critters was believed to patrol Shap Fell after dark. In the 1930s it was reported that the Black Dog was seen running in front of cars on the A6, which passes over Shap Fell. Several fatal accidents occurred during icy and snowy weather on the Shap Fell stretch of the A6 and it was said each was preceded by an appearance of the fateful Black Dog.

GHOSTS ON THE MARCH

Anon appears a brave, a gorgeous show
Of horsemen shadows, moving to and fro.
William Wordsworth

In the early 18th century an extraordinary vision was seen on
the heights of Souther Fell – a phantom army. It was seen on
several occasions. The incident is ably described in *The History
of Cumberland* by William Hutchison, published in the 1790s:

'On midsummer eve, 1735, a servant in the employ of William
Lancaster, of Blakehills, half a mile from Souterfell, related that
he saw the east side of the mountain, towards the summit,
covered with a regular marching army for above an hour
together. They consisted of distinct bodies of troops, which
appeared to proceed from an eminence in the north end, and
marched over a niche in the top, but as no other person in the
neighbourhood had seen a similar appearance, he was
discredited and laughed at.

'A few years after, on midsummer eve also, between the hours
of eight and nine, William Lancaster himself imagined that
several gentlemen were following their horses at a distance, as if
they had been hunting; and taking them for such, paid no regard
to it till about ten minutes after, again turning his head towards
the place, they appear to be mounted, and a vast army following,
five in rank, crowding over the same place, where the servant
said he saw them two years before.

'He then called his family, who all agreed in the same opinion; and what was most extraordinary, he frequently observed that someone of the file would quit the ranks, and seemed to stand in a fronting posture, as if he was observing and regulating the order of their march, or taking account of the numbers, and after some time appeared to return full-gallop to the station he had left, which they never failed to do as often as they quitted their lines, and the figure that did so was generally one of the middlemost men in the rank. As it grew later, they seemed more regardless of the discipline, and rather had the appearance of people riding from a market, than an army, though they continued crowding on, and marching off, as long as there was light to see them.'

Ten years later the 'horseman shadows' (as Wordsworth calls them) were seen again. After the event, the year struck the observers as significant, for 1745 marked the Jacobite Rebellion, when armies of Scots, rallying behind the standard of 'Bonnie Prince Charlie', invaded northern England. The account of this later appearance comes from *Tales and Legends of the English Lakes* by Wilson Armistead, published in 1891:

'This phenomenon was no more observed till the remarkably serene midsummer evening which preceded the last Scotch rebellion. The parties who had witnessed it on the previous occasion, having been much ridiculed for their report, were determined to call a greater number of witnesses of this strange phenomenon; and having first observed it rigidly, and with great caution themselves, and being fully assured they were not deceived as to the actual appearances, they convened about twenty-six persons from different places in the neighbourhood to bear testimony to the existence of the fact. These all affirmed, and attested before a magistrate, that they saw a similar appearance to that just described, but not conducted with the same regularity, having also the appearance of carriages interspersed.

'The numbers of the troops were incredible, for they filled lengthways nearly half a mile, and continued so in a brisk march of above an hour, and would probably have done so much longer had not the darkness of approaching night intervened.'

It has been suggested that what was being witnessed were examples of a phenomenon known as a 'Spectre of the Brocken'. Named after the alpine peak where it was first recorded, the 'spectre' is a shadow thrown onto low clouds and mists. Shadows of mountain climbers can become greatly magnified and hang in the air in a weirdly impressive way. An explanation offered at the time was that the 1745 apparition was a shadow of a Jacobite army carrying out manoeuvres somewhere on the other side of the mountain, but the presence of such a company was never substantiated and wouldn't explain the apparent presence of carriages. Nor, of course, would it explain the earlier appearances.

Phantom armies have been reported throughout the British Isles, especially during the turbulent days of the Civil War. Several battlefields are said to be haunted by those who died there or by the sounds of fighting. However, those seen in the 17th and 18th centuries were presumed to be ghosts of the future, omens of conflicts to come. This is how the 1745 sighting of an army on Souther Fell was afterwards considered. A similar phenomenon also took place on Helvellyn. This phantom army was witnessed in July, 1644, the day before the Battle of Marston Moor in Yorkshire. It was afterwards believed to have been an omen of that decisive Parliamentarian victory.

A phantom army was seen marching over Helvellyn in the 17th century.
Stewart Smith Photography/Shutterstock

An old illustration of the phenomenon known as a 'Spectre of the Brocken', in which shadows are thrown onto low cloud. It was suggested such a phenomenon might explain the shadowy army seen on several occasions marching over Southern Fell

THE CROGLIN VAMPIRE

Stories of vampires are rare in Britain and not very convincing. The stronghold of vampire legend is Eastern Europe. Although much doubt has been expressed over the years regarding the following account of an alleged vampire in Cumbria, it has become a classic of British folklore and it would be remiss not to include it here.

The scene is an ancient house called Croglin Grange, described as 'very curious' because it had never had a second storey built on to it and was therefore unusually long and low. The story appears in one of the volumes of autobiography and family history published by writer and artist Augustus Hare. Hare enjoyed ghost stories and his memoirs contain a goodly number that were told to him (one reviewer drily remarked: 'Mr Hare's ghosts are rather more interesting than his lords or his middle-class people.'). The story was told to Hare by a Captain Fisher, whose family had owned Croglin Grange for centuries. Too cramped for the Fishers, by the 19th century the house was let to tenants. The first of these were two brothers and a sister. Captain Fisher takes up the tale:

'The winter was spent most happily by the new inmates of Croglin Grange, who shared in all the little social pleasures of the district, and made themselves very popular. In the following summer there was one day which was dreadfully, annihilatingly hot. The brothers lay under the trees with their books, for it was too hot for any active occupation. This sister sat in the veranda and worked, or tried to work, for in the intense sultriness of that summer day, work was next to impossible. They dined early, and after dinner they still sat out in the veranda, enjoying the cool air which came with evening, and they watched the sun set, and the moon rise over the belt of trees which separated the grounds from the churchyard, seeing it mount the heavens till the long shadows from the shrubbery fell as if embossed, so vivid and distinct were they.

'When they separated for the night, all retiring to their rooms on the ground-floor (for, as I said, there was no upstairs in that house), the sister felt that the heat was still so great that she could not sleep, and having fastened her window, she did not close the shutters – in that very quiet place it was not necessary – and, propped against the pillows, she still watched the wonderful, the marvellous beauty of that summer night. Gradually she became aware of two lights, two lights which flickered in and out in the belt of trees which separated the lawn from the churchyard, and, as her gaze became fixed upon them, she saw them emerge, fixed in a dark substance, a definite ghastly *something*, which seemed every moment to become nearer, increasing in size and substance as it approached. Every now and then it was lost for a moment in the long shadows which stretched across the lawn from the trees, and then it emerged larger than ever, and still coming on – on.

'As she watched it, the most uncontrollable horror seized her. She longed to get away, but the door was close to the window and the door was locked on the inside, and while she was unlocking it she must be for an instant nearer to *it*. She longed to scream, but her voice seemed paralysed, her tongue glued to the roof of her mouth. Suddenly – she could never explain why afterwards – the terrible object seemed to turn to one side, seemed to be going round the house, not to be coming to her at all, and immediately she jumped out of bed and rushed to the door, but as she was unlocking it she heard scratch, scratch, scratch, upon the window, and saw a hideous brown face with flaming eyes glaring in at her. She rushed back to the bed, but the creature continued to scratch, scratch, scratch upon the window. She felt a sort of mental comfort that the window was securely fastened on the inside. Suddenly the scratching sound ceased and a kind of pecking sound took its place. Then, in her agony, she became aware that the creature was unpicking the lead!

'The noise continued, and a diamond pane of glass fell into the room. Then a long bony finger of the creature came in and turned the handle of the window, and the window opened, and the creature came in; and it came across the room, and her terror was so great that she could not scream, and it came up to the bed, and it twisted its long, bony fingers into her hair, and it dragged her head over the side of the bed, and – it bit her violently in the throat.

'As it bit her, her voice was released, and she screamed with all her might and main. Her brothers rushed out of their rooms, but the door was locked on the inside. A moment was lost while they got a poker and broke it open. Then the creature had already escaped through the window, and the sister, bleeding violently from a wound in the throat, was lying unconscious over the side of the bed. One brother pursued the creature, which fled before him through the moonlight with gigantic strides, and eventually seemed to disappear over the wall into the churchyard. Then he rejoined his brother by the sister's bedside. She was dreadfully hurt, and the wound was a very definite one, but she was of strong disposition, not either given to romance or superstition, and when she came to herself she said, "What has happened is most extraordinary and I am very much hurt. It seems inexplicable, but of course there *is* an explanation, and we must wait for it. It will turn out that a lunatic has escaped from some asylum and found his way here."

'The wound healed, and she appeared to get well, but the doctor who was sent for would not believe that she could bear so terrible a shock so easily, and insisted that she must have change, mental and physical; so her brothers took her to Switzerland. Being a sensible girl, when she went abroad, she threw herself at once into the interests of the country she was in. She dried plants, she made sketches, she went up mountains, and, as autumn came on, she was the person who urged that they should return to Croglin Grange. "We have taken it", she said, "for seven years, and we have only been there one; and we shall always find it difficult to let a house which is only one storey high, so we had better return there; lunatics do not escape every day." As she urged it, the brothers wished nothing better, and the family returned to Cumberland.

'From there being no upstairs in the house, it was impossible to make any great changes in their arrangements. The sister occupied the same room, but it was unnecessary to say she always closed the shutters, which, however, as in many old houses, always left one top of the pane uncovered. The brothers moved, and occupied a room together exactly opposite that of their sister, and they always kept loaded pistols in their room. The winter passed most peacefully and happily. In the following March the sister was suddenly awakened by a sound she remembered only too well – scratch, scratch upon the window, and, looking up, she saw, climbed up to the topmost pane of the window, the same hideous brown, shrivelled face, with glaring eyes, looking in at her.

'This time she screamed as loud as she could. Her brothers rushed out of their room with pistols, and out of the front door. The creature was already scudding away across the lawn. One of the brothers fired and hit it in the leg, but still with the other leg it continued to make way, scrambled over the wall into the churchyard, and seemed to disappear into a vault which belonged to a family long extinct.

'The next day the brothers summoned all the tenants of Croglin Grange, and in their presence the vault was opened. A horrible scene revealed itself. The vault was full of coffins; they had been broken open, and their contents, horribly mangled and distorted, were scattered over the floor. One coffin alone remained intact. Of that the lid had been lifted, but still lay loose upon the coffin. They raised it, and there, brown, withered, shrivelled, mummified, but quite entire, was the same hideous figure which had looked in at the windows of Croglin Grange, with the marks of a recent pistol-shot in the leg; and they did the only thing that can lay a vampire – they burnt it.'

In this eerie yarn's favour is that it was set down before vampire-fever took hold of Britain: the final volume of Augustus Hare's autobiography was published in 1896, a year before the publication of Bram Stoker's *Dracula* (not that *Dracula* was the first vampire story in English but it was the first to really grab the public's imagination). Very much against it is that no house of the name of Croglin Grange is known to have existed, nor does there appear to be one in the area answering its description. Charles Harper pointed this out in his 1907 book on *Haunted Houses*, stressing that neither Croglin Low nor High Farms, the only houses of any age or size with a similar name, lack a second storey. Both are situated near the village of Croglin, north of Kirkoswald, but neither of them is close to a churchyard.

Harper reproduces a sketch of Croglin Low Hall, however, and by so doing unwittingly seems to have linked the farm to the story, despite his assurance to the contrary. Today even the British Listed Buildings website notes of Croglin Low Hall: 'Best known for its association with the Croglin Vampire'!

*Charles Harper made this drawing of Croglin Low Hall for his book
on Haunted Houses, first published in 1907. He states quite categorically
that the house is not the one allegedly visited by the Croglin Vampire but
that hasn't stopped it being associated with the story ever since.*

TWO HORRID MURDERS

It's a familiar theme in British folklore that dramatic incidents,
particularly violent death, can create echoes down the ages in the
form of apparitions and other ghostly goings-on. We have already
seen a number of examples of this belief in *Cumbrian Ghost Stories*. It's
frequently a case of 'murder will out' in ghost-lore, and the more
gruesome the murder, the more likely it is to linger in folk memory
and survive as a ghost.

An especially brutal act took place along the line at Maryport
Railway Station in the 19th century. Not long after the station had
been built, a young couple were making their way over a bridge

across the line when an appalling tragedy took place. We must assume that they were in the midst of a fearful row. Perhaps the husband had felt trapped by his marriage and resented his bride and their new baby. Whatever the reason, his next act was one of a madman. He snatched their new baby, being tenderly held in his wife's arms, and threw it off the bridge.

A train was hurtling down the track and the baby fell into its path. As the engine roared into a tunnel, the child was killed instantly. Its father soon joined it in eternity, on the end of a rope. After this shocking event, local people began to speak of hearing a baby crying near the railway bridge. Often this eerie sound was detected just as a train was entering the tunnel, as if commemorating the exact circumstances of the infant's death. However, as Darren Ritson points out in his *Supernatural North* (Amberley 2009), the 'crying' could simply have been an odd acoustic effect caused by vibration or perhaps air or steam escaping through a flaw in the stone work as a train howled through the tunnel. At any rate, this pathetic little ghost hasn't been reported for some years.

No less horrible, but even more gruesome, is the murder alleged to have taken place at Overwater Hall, near Ireby. Overwater Hall is an attractive Georgian house, standing above a lake and ornamented with mock castellations. It is now a country house hotel.

Legend has it an early owner of the house brought back from his plantations in Jamaica a woman, although not necessarily a wife. Whoever she was, wife or mistress, the new squire of Overwater soon tired of her. The poor woman pleaded with him not to cast her aside. Pretending to make up with her, the villain lured her out in a boat on Overwater tarn and there tried to drown her. He shoved her out of the boat but the frantic woman clutched on to the side. Finding it impossible to loosen her grip for more than a few seconds before she caught hold again, the wretch took out his dagger and hacked off her hands. She sank beneath the crimsoning waters and he rowed calmly back to shore.

Such savagery could not go unpunished, however, and although the squire escaped the notice of the law, the anguished spirit of the murdered woman returned to ensure he would not be able to forget his cruel deed and never know peace of mind again. Her ghastly apparition appeared at night at the doors and windows of the house banging on the glass with the gory, handless stumps of her arms.

This grim apparition has thankfully not been seen for some time but the Overwater Hall Hotel may still be haunted by the same woman. There have been a number of sightings of a female phantom passing through rooms 3 and 4, which were originally one room. It's possible the original chamber was the master bedroom of the house. If so this is where the squire would have slept and this would explain the ghost's presence here. Today, however, she is a quiet presence, glimpsed strolling through the rooms, unhindered by the inconvenience of the intervening wall.

Other **GHOST STORIES** for you to enjoy from
BRADWELL BOOKS

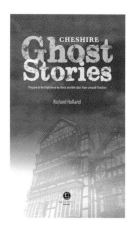

More **GHOST STORIES** from
BRADWELL BOOKS on next page

BRADWELL
BOOKS